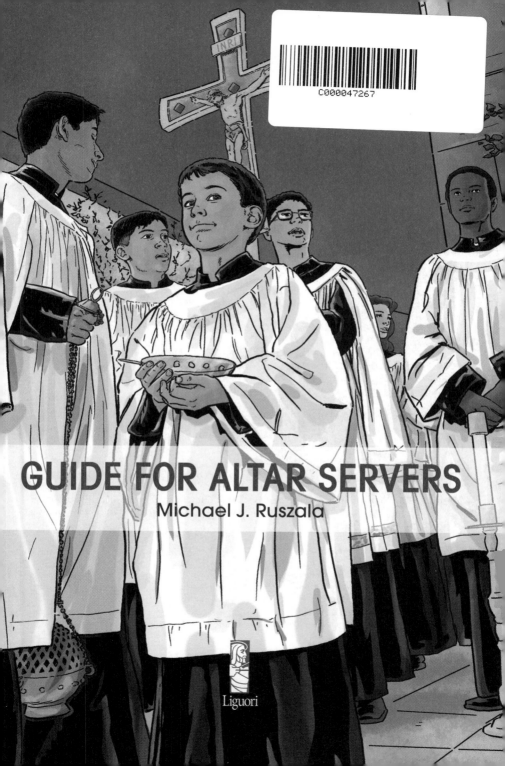

GUIDE FOR ALTAR SERVERS
Michael J. Ruszala

Liguori

Imprimi Potest: Stephen T. Rehrauer, CSsR, Provincial, Denver Province, the Redemptorists

Imprimatur: "In accordance with CIC 827, permission to publish has been granted on June 19, 2017, by the Most Reverend Mark S. Rivituso, Auxiliary Bishop, Archdiocese of St. Louis. Permission to publish is an indication that nothing contrary to Church teaching is contained in this work. It does not imply any endorsement of the opinions expressed in the publication; nor is any liability assumed by this permission."

Published by Liguori Publications, Liguori, MO 63057.
To order, call 800-325-9521, or visit Liguori.org.

p ISBN 978-0-7648-2722-8
e ISBN 978-0-7648-7134-4

Library of Congress Cataloging-in-Publication Data
Names: Ruszala, Michael J., author.
Title: Guide for altar servers / by Michael J. Ruszala.
Description: First Edition. Liguori : Liguori Publications, 2017.
   Includes bibliographical references.
Identifiers: LCCN 2017028566 (print) I LCCN 2017030068 (ebook) I ISBN
   9780764871344 (ebook) I ISBN 9780764827228
Subjects: LCSH: Acolytes—Catholic Church—Handbooks, manuals, etc.
Classification: LCC BX1915 (ebook) I LCC BX1915 .R87 2017 (print) I DDC
   264/.02—dc23
LC record available at https://lccn.loc.gov/2017028566

Liguori Publications, a nonprofit corporation, is an apostolate of the Redemptorists. To learn more about the Redemptorists, visit Redemptorists.com.

Cover image: Catholic News Service
Cover design: Lorena Mitre Jimenez and Jeff Albrecht
Interior design and production: Wendy Barnes and John Krus
Illlustrations: Jeff Albrecht
Product development team: Mary Wuertz von Holt, Chuck Healy, and August Sexauer

Printed in the United States of America

21 20 19 18 17 / 5 4 3 2 1 * First Edition

Contents

Welcome!

You've signed up to be an altar server. Way to go! Why did you choose to become an altar server? Maybe your religious-education teacher said you'd be good at it. Maybe you had friends who signed up. Maybe your parents asked you to think about it. You may not realize it, but there's another reason, too. God has called you to be an altar server. Often, God speaks to us through other people or through a strong desire he gives us.

Many altar servers remember their service their whole life. Altar serving is special because you are so close to what Jesus is doing. At Mass, Jesus himself is leading his people in prayer. He speaks his word to the people and becomes really present in the Eucharist. Mass is very holy. As an **altar server**, you'll serve the priest and other people at Mass. You will help to make it go smoothly for them. In this pamphlet, words in red are defined in the glossary and sometimes in the text as well, while some italicized words may be new to you and are defined in the text.

Altar Servers and Acolytes

For centuries, the service now performed by altar servers was done by acolytes. An **acolyte** is a member of the ministry in the Church. The word means "attendant" or "follower." Some parishes still have acolytes, but the role is usually held by **seminarians**. Seminarians are men studying to become a deacon or priest. Most parishes have altar servers who perform the duties of acolytes. But altar servers don't distribute holy Communion like acolytes can. The patron saints of altar servers are St. John Berchmans and St. Tarcisius. They were both acolytes.

Being an altar server can be fun. It's also serious business. So let's get ready.

Getting Ready at Home

Looking Your Best

Look your best for Mass. You know the routine! Wash your hands and face. Brush your teeth. Neatly comb or style your hair. If your hair is long, hold it together with a band or clip. Candles and loose hair don't mix.

You'll be wearing a **vestment** as an altar server. But still dress nicely for Mass when you're serving. Bold words or bright patterns might still show through the vestments. Solid colors are a good choice. A white shirt or blouse is even better!

Boys: Consider a polo shirt and khakis. A dress shirt and pants is another good choice. A white dress shirt is especially classy. Also, wear dress shoes instead of sports shoes or sandals.

Girls: Wear a dress shirt or blouse with a skirt or nice pants (no jeans), or wear a dress. Before you head out the door, put on a pair of closed-toe dress shoes with a low heel. Sandals, sports shoes, and high heels are not good footwear choices for altar serving.

Being on Time

People are counting on you to be there to help with Mass. It's important to come early, before Mass starts. Plan on being about fifteen minutes early.

If you're serving at a morning Mass rather than an evening Mass, set the alarm clock to get up on time. When should your alarm go off? Think about how long it takes you to eat breakfast and get ready for church. Also think about how far the church is from where you live.

Make sure your parents know when you're supposed to be at church. Also, only sign up for Mass times that you and your ride will be able to make.

Preparing Spiritually

God's Forgiveness

When was the last time you visited a friend's house? You know it's important to be considerate to your friend and his or her family when you are in their home. Likewise, we should get our hearts ready to meet Jesus at Mass. When we are unkind, we hurt God and others. At Mass we pray, "Lord, have mercy." We receive God's forgiveness. This is for our everyday faults, or **venial sins**. For serious, or **mortal sins**, we must make a good confession before we receive holy Communion. Many parishes offer the sacrament of reconciliation on Saturday afternoons. You could also ask a priest to meet with you at a convenient time for the sacrament. Just before Mass isn't a good time, though.

Fasting

Altar servers receive Communion at Mass. Communion is very special. It is not ordinary food. It is Jesus. That's why we fast for an hour before receiving Communion. We don't eat, drink, or chew gum. Water and medicine are fine, though.

Prayer

Before Mass, raise your thoughts to God. Sometimes the ministers helping at Mass pray together beforehand. Think to yourself what you want to pray for. Maybe you want to pray for your grandmother. Maybe you want to pray for help with school.

Use this prayer or your own words:

Lord, thank you for calling me to serve you at the altar.
Help me to sense your presence at Mass.
Help me to grow in serving you and others.
I ask this in Jesus' name. Amen.

Setting an Example for All

As an altar server, you set an example for all. Younger children look to you as well. Always be a good example while serving.

- Walk at a slow but steady pace. There's no need to be nervous.

  - Fold your hands when not holding or carrying something.

  - Stand or sit up straight.

  - Cover your mouth if you need to yawn, sneeze, or cough.

  - Keep quiet when it's not time to speak. But feel free to laugh at the priest's jokes in the homily.

- Listen to the readings, the homily, and the prayers.

- Learn and say the responses out loud. The missalette will help you.

Just Before Mass

Learning Your Way Around the Sacristy

When you come to serve, you'll usually go to the **sacristy**. This is the room where the priest gets ready for Mass. The sacrarium may also be there. The **sacrarium** is the sink that drains into the ground for holy water to be disposed of carefully. It's used for washing the sacred vessels.

There may be another room for altar servers. Usually the schedule is posted in that room or in the sacristy. Be sure to find it! Also look for the *usher closet* and *choir closet* at your parish. These are storage rooms for certain ministries.

Vestments

Have you ever been on a sports team or in a play? Did you wear a uniform or a costume? What you wore depended on what you were doing. At Mass, the priest, deacon, and servers wear vestments over their clothes. Different ministers wear different vestments. Wearing vestments shows that Mass is holy. The vestments are usually kept in the sacristy. Be familiar with the vestments that altar servers may wear:

- An **alb** is a flowing white robe. It reminds us of the white we wore at baptism. Putting on an alb is like putting on Christ. It also reminds us of heaven. At many parishes, altar servers wear albs. Priests and deacons wear albs under other vestments.

- A **cincture** is a cord or rope. It ties around your waist like a belt. The cincture keeps the alb in place. It is either white or the liturgical color for that Mass.

- A **cassock** is a tighter-fitting robe. It stretches to your feet and has long sleeves. It is usually closed by a long row of buttons. The **surplice** is a fancy white garment. It fits like a shirt. The surplice is worn over a cassock. It goes down only to the waist. At some parishes, altar servers wear a cassock and surplice instead of an alb.

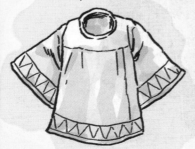

Good to Know

Your parish should have a few albs of different lengths. Look for one that lands just above your ankles. If it drags on the floor, it's too big. You might trip. If it barely covers your knees, it's too small. If you have trouble finding the right one, ask the priest or another altar server for help. If they can't find one, ask another minister or the sacristan.

These next vestments are for priests or deacons. It is helpful for you to know them:

- A **stole** goes over a priest's or deacon's alb. The priest's stole hangs down both sides in the front. It looks a little like a scarf. The deacon wears a stole over the left shoulder and to the side. This way, it looks like a sash.

- A **chasuble** goes over a priest's stole. The word *chasuble* means "little house." Its color depends on the liturgical season. It has no sleeves. A deacon may wear a **dalmatic** over his stole. This vestment is similar to the chasuble but has long sleeves.

Liturgical Colors

Does your family like to decorate for holidays throughout the year? As Catholics, we celebrate Church seasons. We mark special occasions with colors and symbols. The color for many of the vestments depends on the liturgical season.

Violet or **purple** is used during Advent and Lent. Advent prepares us for Christmas. Lent prepares us for Easter. Violet or purple in the Church symbolizes penance and royalty.

Gold or **white** marks the Christmas and Easter seasons. It's also used for certain feast days and special occasions. It may be used for funerals as well. This color symbolizes light, purity, and joy.

Green is used during Ordinary Time. That's when we hear stories from the Gospels about Jesus' teaching and ministry. This color symbolizes growth.

Red symbolizes blood. It also reminds us of the fire of the Holy Spirit. It is used on days marking Christ's passion and death. Red is also used on celebrations of the apostles, Gospel writers, and martyrs. On Pentecost, it reminds us of the Holy Spirit.

Rose is a color of joyful expectation. It may be used on the third Sunday of Advent. It may also be used on the fourth Sunday of Lent.

Black is an option for funerals and Masses for the dead. It's rarely used, though.

Lighting the Candles

Altar servers are often asked to light the candles before Mass, though sometimes this is done by a sacristan. The **sacristan** doesn't serve at Mass but helps with the preparations.

To light the candles, use a **candlelighter**, which is a long metal device with a wick for lighting candles. It may also have a snuffer to extinguish candles. First, safely light the wick of the candlelighter while you are in the sacristy using a match or torch. Next, carefully and slowly walk to the altar and light at least one candle on either side of the altar. You may need to hold the wick of the candlelighter to the wick of the candle for a few moments before the candle lights. Some parishes use a simple lighter or torch instead of a candlelighter to light the candles.

The priest or deacon may direct you to light other candles, according to the preferences of your parish. For instance, during the Easter season, the **Easter** (or **paschal**) **candle** is always lit for Mass. It is a large, white, decorated candle that symbolizes the light of Christ. It is blessed and first lit at the Easter Vigil Mass. The Easter candle is placed near the ambo (podium) or in the sanctuary during the Easter season.

What if the Candle Won't Light?

If you're having trouble lighting a candle after a few good tries, ask a priest or a sacristan for help. Always remember fire safety.

If the wick is buried under a little wax and there's time, try to free the wick and then light it. Is the lighter or torch out of fluid? Get another one.

Entrance Procession

Ready to begin Mass? After putting on the vestments, the ministers wait for the **procession**. The procession usually starts at the **narthex**. This is the area between the main entrance and the worship space. Your parish may call it the **gathering space** or **vestibule**. It is the entrance to this holy place.

Do you like parades? As you know, police officers and firefighters don't just walk any way they like in a parade. They march in a particular order. They usually march behind their banner or a flag. At Mass, the ministers walk into church in an orderly way as well. This is called the entrance procession. It takes place during the entrance chant.

Altar servers lead the way, in this order:

1. Any altar servers with **incense** (perfumed smoke)

2. An altar server carrying the cross, known as a *cross bearer*

3. Any servers carrying candles or torches

4. Any servers not carrying anything

5. Any servers carrying a banner

The other ministers and clergy follow like this:

1. Any **lay** (not ordained) ministers—extraordinary ministers of holy Communion, lectors (readers), and so on

2. Any deacons

3. Any priests or bishops **concelebrating** (offering the Mass with the main *presider*)

4. The **celebrant** (the priest or bishop leading or presiding at the Mass), who is always last

The **nave** is the main body of the church's worship space. It is where the people sit. **Sanctuary** means "holy place." It is a raised area reserved for clergy and ministers. It may also be called the **chancel**. In some older churches, it may be set off by an *altar rail*. In the entrance procession, you'll be walking through the nave toward the sanctuary.

CELEBRANT

CONCELEBRATING PRIEST

DEACON

ALTAR SERVERS
CARRYING CANDLES

CROSS BEARER

The **altar** is at the center of the sanctuary. It is the table of sacrifice where the Eucharist is celebrated. During Mass, we bow to the altar whenever we pass in front of it. When the procession reaches the altar, bow fully at the waist. But there's an exception. If you're carrying something, then only bow your head. The rules are the same for the final procession.

Genuflecting Toward the Tabernacle

A **tabernacle** is a special decorated box where the Eucharist is kept. A **sanctuary lamp** burns nearby to show that Christ is present. Is your church's tabernacle right behind the altar? If so, ministers may **genuflect** in the processions before and after Mass instead of bowing. This means they may go down on their right knee and make the sign of the cross. Follow what the ministers do at your parish for the procession. People carrying something in a procession still only bow their heads. Notice that the people also genuflect when they go into and out of their **pews** (bench).

Good to Know

The main *crucifix* or *cross* is placed in the sanctuary. If your parish's *processional cross* is the main cross, it likely has a stand. If it's a smaller or secondary cross, it is placed out of view. The altar server who carries the processional cross puts it in its proper place once the procession reaches the altar.

The *chair* for the celebrating priest or bishop is in the sanctuary, too. Seats are nearby for other clergy and for the altar servers. Go to your seat, but don't sit down yet.

Introductory Rites

After the opening blessing, the priest may say a few words. He continues with the *penitential act*. We pray either "Lord, have mercy ..." or "I confess to almighty God...." On Sundays and certain holy days, we sing or say the "Gloria," which begins: "Glory to God in the highest." But the "Gloria" is left out during Advent and Lent. It's not hard to memorize. We hear it often at Mass. The tune helps us remember the words.

Next, one of the altar servers holds open a large book called **The Roman Missal**. It is placed on a table near the altar servers before Mass starts. From it, the priest reads the opening prayer. This prayer is called the **Collect**. He begins by saying, "Let us pray." Here are a few tips:

- Hold the book away from yourself at chest level. Rest it on your forearms or chest so the priest can read it.

- Stand at a slight angle from the priest to avoid blocking the view of others.

- Ribbons in the book should be set to the right places beforehand. Stand still if the priest needs to open or fix the pages.

Liturgy of the Word

The next part of the Mass is called the **Liturgy** of the Word. We listen carefully to God's word in the Bible. Some of the stories may be familiar to you. Think about the people mentioned in the readings. Why are they important? What did you find interesting or confusing about the readings? What does God want you to learn or do?

The Scriptures are read from an **ambo**, which is located to the side of the altar. An ambo is a tall stand or podium. Your parish may call it a *lectern* or *pulpit*. The book with all the readings for Mass is called the **Lectionary**. It is kept on the ambo. There is also an ornate **Book of the Gospels**. It has only the Gospel readings. The *Book of the Gospels* may be carried in during the entrance procession by a deacon or lector. It is then displayed on the altar. When it is time to read the Gospel, it will be taken to the ambo by the deacon or priest.

On Sundays and holy days, the *first reading* usually comes from the Old Testament. Sometimes it is from the Acts of the Apostles. On weekdays, the first reading can also be from the New Testament. The first reading has a similar theme to the Gospel reading.

The *responsorial psalm* is the people's response to God's message. The congregation repeats the response between the verses. They may sing or say it.

On Sundays and holy days, there is also a *second reading*. This comes from the New Testament of the Bible.

Before the Gospel, we sing or say "Alleluia," which means "Praise God!" During Lent, another *Gospel acclamation* is used.

The *Gospel reading* is shown the greatest reverence at Mass. This is because it tells what Jesus said and did. Only a priest or deacon may proclaim the Gospel at Mass. For the other readings, the people sit. But for the Gospel, everyone stands.

You may have a special role in showing reverence to the Gospel. At some parishes, altar servers may process to the ambo during the Gospel acclamation. These altar servers hold candles or torches. They lead the way for the priest or deacon. If incense is used, an altar server with incense may lead the way. Follow the instructions you are given at your parish.

Next, the priest or deacon explains the readings in the *homily*.

At school or public events, citizens often recite the Pledge of Allegiance. Scouts stand and say the Scout oath together at every meeting. At Mass, all the faithful recite the Nicene or Apostles' Creed as a statement or *profession of faith*. It reminds us what we believe. It is also a prayer of faith in God's word. Use your missalette or a pew card until you know the words by heart.

Do you know someone who could especially use God's help? In the *Universal Prayer*, the people ask for God's help and grace. These *general intercessions* are offered for the leaders of the Church, for the world, for the sick, and for the needs of the community. This is sometimes called the *Prayer of the Faithful*.

Liturgy of the Eucharist

Now it's time for the *preparation of the gifts*. Do you remember what card or gift you got your parents for Mother's Day and Father's Day? You showed them you loved them and were thankful to them. At the **offertory**, the people offer God simple gifts of bread and wine. He will change these gifts for us into the Body and Blood of Christ.

The altar is also prepared at this time. Some altar servers may help to prepare the altar, while some may go with the priest to accept the gifts from the people. Know beforehand whether you will walk down with the priest or help at the altar. If you walk down, he may pass the gifts to you. How to prepare the altar is discussed next.

Incense may be used again at this point. The priest first incenses the gifts, the cross, and the altar. Then he may give the incense to a deacon or altar server. This minister then incenses the priest and the people. If you are asked to do this, the deacon or priest will teach you how before Mass. For more information on using incense, see the section "Working With Incense" under "Special Celebrations."

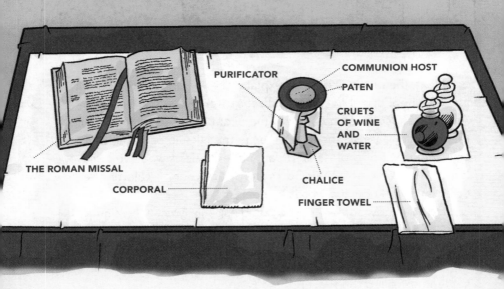

PURIFICATOR

COMMUNION HOST

PATEN

CRUETS OF WINE AND WATER

THE ROMAN MISSAL

CORPORAL

CHALICE

FINGER TOWEL

Things Used to Prepare the Altar

You can be more helpful if you know what everything is called. **Sacred vessels** contain the Body and Blood of Christ. They should be treated with respect. You may see them on the

credence table, which is a small side table. You may be asked to carry them to the altar when the altar is prepared. Be able to identify them.

The **paten** looks like a small plate. It is usually covered in gold or silver. The paten carries the large host that the priest holds up while saying, "This is my Body...." The **ciborium** is a bowllike vessel for carrying many hosts that become the precious Body. It usually has a lid that can be taken off.

The **chalice** is the priest's large ornate cup for the wine that becomes the precious Blood. There may be smaller and simpler **Communion cups** for the people, too. Nearby are small linen cloths called **purificators**. Purificators go with the chalice and Communion cups. They are used to wipe the edges. Afterward, the purificators are put aside to be washed in a special way.

Preparing the Altar

The priest or deacon prepares the altar at the preparation of the gifts. The priest may do this before he receives the gifts, or he may receive the gifts while the deacon prepares the altar. If you help, here are the basic steps:

1. Unfold the corporal gently on the altar. Put it just in front of the place where the priest will stand.

Vessels are placed on a white linen called a **corporal**. This cloth is laid on top of the main altar cloth. The word *corporal* refers to Christ's body. Bread and wine to be **consecrated** must be placed on the corporal. A folded corporal may be kept in a **burse**, which is a special pouch.

2. Take the chalice, paten, and a purificator. Place them on the corporal.

Sometimes chalices and Communion cups are covered before Mass starts. A stiff square cover goes over them. This is called a **pall**. Then a cloth veil may be draped on top.

Some parishes use a large pitcher, or **flagon**, of wine for Communion. You may sometimes be asked to fill the Communion cups with the wine from the flagon.

3. Set *The Roman Missal* on the altar where the priest can easily read it.

4. Set out the Communion cups and purificators. Follow any other instructions as well.

Sometimes Communion is taken out to the sick who can't go to Mass. The host for a homebound person is placed in a very small vessel with a lid. This is called a **pyx**. It is usually shaped like a host and can carry several hosts if needed.

The Hand-washing Rite

After the priest has received the gifts of bread and wine and is back at the altar, it is time for the hand-washing rite. One or two servers help with this rite. The hand-washing rite is about how the priest is washed from sin before celebrating the Eucharist.

There is a small pitcher of water on the credence table. This is called a **cruet**. You need a cruet of water and a **lavabo** bowl to catch the water. You also need a **finger towel** for the priest to dry his hands.

1. Take a finger towel, lavabo bowl, and cruet of water from the credence table. Drape the towel over your forearm so you can hold the cruet in one hand and the bowl in the other.

2. The priest pours the wine into his chalice. Then he pours a drop of water into the wine.

3. After offering some prayers, the priest places his hands over the lavabo bowl. Pour a little water over his hands into the bowl. The priest then dries his hands with the towel.

4. Return the towel, bowl, and cruets to the credence table.

The Eucharistic Prayer

After a few prayers, the priest begins the *eucharistic prayer*. This is the most sacred prayer of the Mass.

Before the *consecration*, everyone sings or says the "Holy, Holy, Holy." Memorize this short and easy prayer.

At some parishes, an altar server rings a bell when the priest lifts the host and chalice at the words of consecration. Ring it the first time after the priest says,

"...this is my Body, which will be given up for you."

Ring the bell again after the priest says,

"...this is the chalice of my Blood....Do this in memory of me."

Then the priest says, "The mystery of faith." The people respond with a *memorial acclamation*. There are three options. All are easy to learn.

The *Communion rite* comes at the end of the Liturgy of the Eucharist:

All say or sing the Lord's Prayer ("Our Father..."). Next is the *rite of peace*. You might shake hands with the other altar servers or ministers. Say to them, "Peace be with you." Then the people sing or say the "Lamb of God." The priest breaks the host, symbolizing Christ's death.

You will stand or line up to receive Communion. Altar servers are among the first. So know where to go.

Return to your place to reflect and pray silently—unless you are given the job of holding a **Communion paten**. This is a paten with a handle. Its purpose is to catch the hosts if they fall during Communion. Hold the Communion paten by the handle. Extend it to just under the chin (if receiving by tongue) or hands (if receiving by hand) of each person receiving. Keep it upright so the crumbs don't fall.

Afterward, hand the Communion paten to the priest or deacon. They will make sure it's purified and cleaned.

Altar servers may be needed again after Communion. They may carry vessels and linens back from the altar to the credence table.

Then the priest may need a server to hold *The Roman Missal* for the *prayer after Communion*.

What if the Precious Blood Is Spilled or the Host Is Dropped?

Ask if your parish has any rules on this matter. Some tips:

If a consecrated host or part of it falls, tell the priest, deacon, or extraordinary minister of holy Communion. They will pick it up and dissolve it properly.

Good to Know

If the precious Blood spills, tell them quickly. To help, bring several purificators to soak it up. These linens will be purified. They will not be thrown away. Then cover the area with dry purificators so no one walks there.

If *unconsecrated* bread or wine falls or spills, clean it up. But don't put them out for the priest to consecrate. Put them in the sacristy or on the credence table. Let a minister or the sacristan know so they can be taken care of and replaced.

Concluding Rites

As an altar server, you may need to hold *The Roman Missal* for the priest to read the final blessing. This may come after any announcements.

When it's time for the final procession, follow the priest's lead when heading out.

All the ministers gather in front of the altar. They face the altar in a certain order. The altar server with the cross stands farthest from the altar. Then when everyone turns around and goes out, the cross will be first. The other servers with candles stand closer to the altar. But they give the priest and deacon room to stand closest to the altar. Then when everyone turns around to go out, the priest will be last in the procession. Again, the lay ministers are between the altar servers and the priest and deacon. The lineup is the same as it was during the entrance procession, but this time going away from the altar.

Wait for the priest to bow or genuflect to the altar. When he does so, everyone bows or genuflects as well. If you're carrying something, just slightly bow your head. Then everyone turns and begins walking out slowly.

After Mass

When Mass is over, say a prayer of thanks like this:

Thank you, Jesus, for the privilege of serving you at Mass today.
Thank you for coming into my heart in holy Communion.
Purify my heart. Guide my actions.
Help me to grow closer to you. Amen.

Hang up your vestments after Mass. Put them where they belong neatly. Put away the cross if you carried it. Otherwise, if you carried a candle, blow it out and put it where it belongs. Your parish may have other duties for tidying up after Mass as well. For instance, you may need to extinguish the candles on the altar.

You have served God and his people. You should feel good about a job well done.

Special Celebrations

Daily Mass or School Mass

A weekday Mass is usually simpler than a Mass on a Sunday or holy day. For instance, there is often only one reading in addition to the Gospel. Sometimes the processions are simpler, too. If the congregation is small, there may not be an offertory or presentation of gifts. There may not even be music. Your parish will give you specific guidelines for daily Masses.

Mass With a Bishop

Serving Mass with a bishop can be exciting. The bishop usually has a priest, deacon, or minister to help him. But you may be needed to carry his miter or crosier. The **miter** is the bishop's tall, pointed headdress. The **crosier** is like a shepherd's staff.

The bishop goes last in a procession. He wears the miter on his head and has the crosier in his hand. His miter- and crosier-bearers follow behind him. They will take his miter and crosier when he enters the sanctuary. Be ready to take them and set them aside.

Under the miter, the bishop wears a skull cap on his head. This is called a **zucchetto**. After the preparation of the gifts, he takes that off as well. If you are called upon to take it from him, gently place it on his chair.

After Communion, the bishop puts his zucchetto back on. You may need to bring it to him. Hand back his miter and crosier before the final blessing.

As usual, the ministers gather in front of the altar for the final procession. The bishop will be closest to the altar. Then when everyone turns around to go out, he will be last in the procession, except for the miter- and crosier-bearers, who will follow him.

Baptisms

Be sure to identify the **baptismal font**. This is a large pool or basin of holy water for baptisms. It may be located near the entrance to the nave of the church. It may also be in a separate room called a *baptistry*. The Easter (paschal) candle will be nearby.

When assisting at a baptism, be ready to help by holding the book for the priest or deacon to read from, as needed.

You may also need to fetch or carry these items:

- the oil of catechumens and sacred chrism (two blessed oils)

- the white garment (if not provided by the family)

- the baptismal candle

Weddings

Wedding Masses are exciting occasions that couples always remember. If there is an entrance procession, the servers and ministers are arranged in the usual order. The wedding party follows. If only the wedding party processes, just take your place in the sanctuary.

The marriage rites come after the homily. You may be needed to hold the ritual book for the priest. Be ready with the aspergillum and holy water bucket for the blessing of rings. This comes after the couple's exchange of vows.

There will be a nuptial blessing over the couple. This comes after the Lord's Prayer and before Communion. The couple is then presented to the people after the prayer after Communion.

Finally, the bride and groom process out. They are followed by the wedding party and then the ministers, in the usual procession order.

Some Catholic weddings are celebrated outside of Mass with a priest or deacon witnessing. In these cases, there will be an entrance procession, a Liturgy of the Word, and the marriage rites. Then there will be a Universal Prayer, the Lord's Prayer, a nuptial blessing, and a dismissal. There will not be a Liturgy of the Eucharist.

Funerals

At a funeral, altar servers can help add dignity to the occasion. Even if you don't know the person who died, show respect for the family and friends. This will help to comfort them.

If there is a casket, it is near the narthex at the beginning of Mass. The procession goes out from the sanctuary to meet it. The priest offers prayers beside it. If there is no casket, this is not done.

The casket is sprinkled with holy water. This recalls the deceased person's baptism. You may need to carry the **aspergillum**, used for sprinkling holy water. Hand it to the priest when needed. There may also be an **aspersorium** (a holy water bucket) to dip it into that you or another altar server may carry.

A pall (white cloth) is draped over the casket. It reminds us of the baptismal garment the person once wore.

You might be asked to carry incense. If so, hand the thurible and incense boat to the priest. He incenses the casket. (See page 39 for more information on working with incense.)

Then the entrance procession continues in the usual way. The casket is rolled in or carried behind the priest. It is placed at the foot of the altar. The family of the deceased may follow and sit in the front pews.

If a burial is to follow, there is a special rite after the prayer after Communion. This is called the *rite of final commendation*. The altar servers stand next to the casket or next to the priest. Find out from the priest beforehand where he would like you to stand. Incense may be used again, and you might be called on to assist as before.

For the final procession, the servers lead the way, followed by the priest. The casket goes last, behind the priest. The family and friends follow the casket.

Benediction

In a **benediction** service, a priest or deacon blesses the people with the Eucharist. The Eucharist is displayed in a **monstrance**. A monstrance is a special stand. It is often golden and sun-shaped. In its center is a circular glass vessel that holds one consecrated host. This vessel is called a **luna**. The benediction usually comes after eucharistic **adoration**. Eucharistic adoration is worshiping Christ in the Eucharist when displayed in the monstrance.

Servers are often needed for benediction. Here are some tips: Process with the priest or deacon to the altar. Genuflect to the monstrance. Then kneel beside him at the foot of the altar. There is a hymn (usually *Tantum Ergo*). At this point, present the thurible and incense boat to the priest or deacon. Then incense the monstrance. After a prayer, present the priest or deacon with a **humeral veil**. Help him to drape it around his shoulders. Hand the clasps to him from behind. The humeral veil goes over his cope. A **cope** is a capelike vestment worn for benediction. The priest or deacon then uses the humeral veil to hold the monstrance. Here, Christ himself offers the blessing. Notice that the priest or deacon does not even touch the monstrance with his hands at this point.

The priest or deacon raises the monstrance for the blessing. He traces the shape of a cross with it very slowly. There are three points to the blessing as usual. There is one for the Father, one for the Son, and one for the Holy Spirit. The thurifer gives a double swing to the thurible at each of the three points. The priest or deacon then kneels down. Help him remove the humeral veil.

There is a hymn (usually "Holy God We Praise Thy Name"). At this, the priest or deacon returns the luna with the host to the tabernacle. Stand at the foot of the altar. The final procession follows in the usual manner.

Working With Incense

Sometimes altar servers get to work with incense. Incense has been used for thousands of years to make a beautifully scented smoke. An altar server responsible for incense is called a **thurifer**. Incense can be used several times at Mass. Often, it's saved for special occasions. The granules of incense are taken from a small metal vessel. This vessel is called an **incense boat**. Then the granules are placed into a metal incense container attached to chains. This is called a **thurible** or **censer**.

If someone or something is incensed at Mass, it is a sign that Christ is present there. Some things that may be incensed are the following:

- the *priest*, who acts as Christ
- the **congregation** (the faithful people in the pews), made holy by their baptisms
- the *Book of the Gospels*, through which God speaks to us
- the *bread and wine* that become Christ's Body and Blood
- the *altar*, the place of sacrifice
- the *cross*
- *the Easter candle*

Before Mass, a charcoal briquette (small brick) is placed in the thurible. It is lit with a lighter in the sacristy. This is done by the priest, deacon, or sacristan, but they may ask for your help. The thurible may be kept on a stand in the sanctuary until needed.

When you are ready to take the thurible, raise the lid by lifting the chains. Don't touch the thurible itself because it is hot. Gently rock the thurible by the chains. The bottom should swing a little below your knees. Hold the chains high enough to avoid the floor.

Carry the incense boat in your other hand. If you're not carrying the boat, place the empty hand over your heart.

Go and stand behind the altar, and wait on the priest's right side. Hand him the incense boat. Then lift the thurible's cover (using the chains). He places the incense inside and blesses it.

Exception: If a deacon is present, first hand him the incense boat. Then hand the thurible to him. He presents them to the priest.

The thurifer (either the deacon or an altar server) may also incense the priest, other ministers, and the assembly. When done, the thurifer places the thurible on its stand.

Your parish will have specific rules about safely extinguishing the incense afterward and cleaning up.

What Happens if...?

When serving at Mass, we have to expect the unexpected. Here are some tips and tricks for when that happens.

...I trip, get hurt, or get sick while serving?

If you trip but are uninjured, just get up as if nothing happened. You can deal with a little pain or soreness. But if you are bleeding, badly bruised, or seriously ill, go to the sacristy for some first aid. Maybe the priest, sacristan, or another adult can help.

...My friend is making me smile or something is distracting me?

First, look away and don't pay attention to it. If it's another server, tell him or her that you need to focus. If you can't help what's going on, add it to your prayer. Sometimes St. Thérèse of the Child Jesus was distracted by others while praying. She would just pray for them.

...I forget to do something?

We all forget now and then. Then we learn and move on. Don't disturb the Mass in trying to correct something.

If you forget to hold the book for the priest, he can take care of it this time. If you forget what to do, follow the lead of an experienced server. Otherwise, briefly and quietly ask that server what to do. If you forget to bow, just bow next time. If you forget the responses, find the words in the pew card or missalette. It's a good idea to set one of these on your pew or seat before Mass. Also, be patient and polite if you are corrected.

Try your best. The more often you serve, the more confident you'll become. You'll even find that when you make mistakes, everything is all right. Altar serving is about God. It's not about what other people think. Carry this confidence into other parts of your life.

...I break something?

Let the sacristan or priest know. If it happens during Mass but isn't essential or dangerous, wait until after Mass.

...I can't serve at a Mass I am scheduled for?

Different parishes have different rules. Some ask you to find your own substitute. Others ask you to contact a member of the parish staff. Either way, it's best to give as much notice as possible.

...I'm asked to serve at another parish?

If you are asked to serve at another parish now and then, find out what differences there may be. You and your family should decide which parish to belong to. You should support that parish through time, talent, and treasure.

...I don't want to be an altar server anymore?

First, you should know your real feelings and reasons.

Do you need a break or want to try another ministry? Tell the person in charge of altar servers. But serve the Masses you're scheduled for. Honor your commitment.

Do you feel embarrassed or unprepared? Are you struggling in your faith? Talk it over with a trusted priest, deacon, teacher, or parent. Like God, your Church is there for you. No matter what you decide, your parish will be thankful for your service.

...I feel really close to God when serving at Mass?

That's wonderful! Altar servers sometimes start to think about how God wants them to ultimately serve in life. This is called a *vocation*. Boys might consider if God is calling them to some day be a priest, deacon, religious brother, husband and father, or generous single person. Girls might consider if God is calling them to be a religious sister, a wife and mother, or a single person serving others. Maybe talk it over with a priest, a parent, or a religious-education teacher.

As a disciple of Jesus, you represent him to the world. You have his Spirit and light within you. When you do your best to serve God and others, you feel good. Take this spirit of service at the altar into the rest of your life!

Activities

Complete these puzzles by writing or finding the terms below.
Look up any words you don't understand.
Most are defined in the glossary.

Crossword

ACROSS

3. raised area around the altar
5. religious garments worn by ministers
7. basic, white vestment symbolizing baptism
8. priestly vestment without sleeves; means "little house"
9. cord fastened around the waist to keep an alb in place

DOWN

1. large, ornate cup for the precious Blood
2. a special locked box for storing consecrated hosts
4. the podium from which the readings are proclaimed
6. a small, platelike vessel for the host
7. the table of sacrifice where the Eucharist is celebrated

Answers are on page 62.

1. Y X P

_____ Y _____

2. M R I C O U B I

C I _____ _____ _____ I U M

3. S E C R E N

_____ _____ _____ S E R

4. G O L F A N

F L A _____ _____ _____

5. L A T C I M A D

D A _____ _____ _____ T I C

6. T R U C E

_____ _____ _____ E T

7. L O R P A R O C

C O R _____ _____ R _____ _____

8. CLUGENEFT

G E N U _____ _____ _____ _____ _____

9. CIFIRORPUTA

P U R _____ _____ _____ _____ _____ T O _____

10. TELBACREN

C E L _____ _____ _____ _____ N _____

CLUES

1. small, round vessel with a lid for carrying Communion to the sick
2. chalice- or bowllike vessel for carrying many hosts
3. metal device used for burning incense; a thurible
4. a large pitcher
5. vestment with sleeves worn by a deacon over his alb
6. a small pitcher
7. linen on which the sacred vessels are set, placed over the altar cloth
8. a gesture of reverence in which one goes down on the right knee
9. small, folded linen for wiping the chalice
10. the main priest or bishop at Mass; the presider

Answers are on page 63.

Word Search

WORD BANK

- lavabo
- bishop
- surplice
- acolyte
- pew
- narthex
- sacristy
- Collect
- cassock

Answers are on page 63.

```
H H P P N P P C S C G C C W Z
V R V Y M A V O M I A T O E B
B F K T L A R C H S O E L P M
O T E S C L B T S S C R L Y I
L Q X I B P B O H I I X E N K
P V K R W B C Z L E P B C T K
I N A C R K O P X W X L T W R
T F H A G X R O B A V A L N G
V W U S J U G L Q J Y U R I A
V C K T S Y A C O L Y T E Z J
K U K R A K D V U U L V H H G
V J S F L B K C O S S A C Q E
Q K L I U O J I O D I W B O I
D P V F Z A D P R H O F R F F
B Z U E L G E O Q T Q R I X Z
```

Find each of the items listed below in your parish:

- ☐ alb
- ☐ altar
- ☐ ambo
- ☐ aspergillum
- ☐ candlelighter
- ☐ chalice / Communion cups
- ☐ ciborium
- ☐ cincture
- ☐ corporal
- ☐ credence table
- ☐ cruet
- ☐ finger towel
- ☐ flagon
- ☐ incense boat
- ☐ lavabo
- ☐ monstrance
- ☐ narthex (gathering space)
- ☐ nave
- ☐ paten
- ☐ purificator
- ☐ sacristy
- ☐ sanctuary
- ☐ sanctuary lamp
- ☐ tabernacle
- ☐ thurible (censer)

Glossary

acolyte: Literally "follower" or "attendant"; an instituted minister traditionally reserved for those in formation to become deacons or priests.

(eucharistic) adoration: Worshiping Christ in the Eucharist, usually in the form of prayer before a host exposed in a monstrance.

alb: The most basic vestment; a white flowing garment symbolizing baptism.

altar: The table of sacrifice where the Eucharist is celebrated.

altar server: A person, often an older boy or girl, who serves at the Mass and other liturgical functions and assists the priest at the altar.

ambo: The podium from which the readings are proclaimed; sometimes called the *lectern* or *pulpit*.

aspergillum: A holy water sprinkler.

aspersorium: A holy water vessel.

baptismal font: a large basin or pool of holy water where baptisms are performed, often located near the entrance to the church nave.

benediction (of the Blessed Sacrament): A liturgical service in which a priest or deacon blesses the people with a consecrated host displayed in a monstrance; adoration often follows.

Book of the Gospels: Ornate book containing the Gospel readings for Mass; often carried in procession.

burse: A pouch or pocket in which a corporal or pyx is stored and carried to and from the altar.

candlelighter: A long metal device with a wick for lighting candles; it may also have a snuffer to extinguish candles; this term also describes the person lighting the candles.

cassock: A tight-fitting robe stretching to the feet. It has long sleeves and is usually fastened by a long row of buttons.

celebrant: The main priest or bishop leading the Mass or other liturgical function. Sometimes called the *presider*.

censer: See **thurible**.

chalice: The priest's large ornate cup for the wine that becomes the precious Blood.

chasuble: A priestly vestment without sleeves that stretches over the arms while allowing the priest to move freely; literally means "little house."

ciborium: A chalicelike or bowllike vessel for carrying a large quantity of hosts which become the precious Body.

cincture: A cord fastened around the waist to keep an alb in place.

Collect: Used in the Mass, the opening prayer to "collect" the minds and hearts of the people.

Communion cups: Cups for people to receive the precious Blood.

Communion paten: A flat plate with a handle placed under the chin or hands of those receiving Communion.

concelebrate: To offer the Mass with the celebrant priest or bishop, as another ordained minister.

congregation: The assembly of baptized Christians; the faithful present at Mass.

consecrate: To make sacred and dedicate for a divine purpose. For example, consecrated bread and wine have become the Body and Blood (Real Presence) of Christ; consecrated men and women have taken religious vows but are not ordained ministers.

cope: A capelike vestment worn by the priest at a benediction service.

corporal: A linen on which the sacred vessels are set, placed over the altar cloth.

credence table: A small side table in the sanctuary.

crosier: The bishop's "shepherd's staff."

cruet: A small pitcher, often made of glass.

dalmatic: A vestment with sleeves worn by a deacon over his alb.

Easter (paschal) candle: A large, decorated candle lit at the Easter Vigil and used in the rite of baptism

finger towel: The towel used for the priest's rite of hand-washing at Mass.

flagon: A large pitcher that holds the wine to be consecrated.

gathering space: See **narthex**.

genuflect: A gesture of reverence in which one goes down on the right knee and makes the sign of the cross.

humeral veil: A vestment that drapes around the shoulders of a deacon or a priest, used to grasp the monstrance in a benediction service.

incense: A material made from plants, spices, oil, and/or gum or resin that is burned for its perfumed smoke in ritual worship and blessings; the original Latin word means "to burn."

incense boat: A small, oblong vessel in which incense is kept until it's moved into the thurible.

Lectionary: The book containing the Scripture (Bible) readings for Mass.

lavabo: A bowl used to catch the water for the priest's rite of handwashing at Mass.

lay (people): Men and women who are neither ordained nor have taken religious vows; members of the *laity*.

liturgy: The Church's "public worship"; the main Catholic liturgy is the Mass, which has two parts: the Liturgy of the Word and the Liturgy of the Eucharist.

luna: A circular, glass, sacred vessel used to display one consecrated host in a monstrance.

miter: The bishop's tall, pointed headdress.

monstrance: An ornate stand, often shaped like a sunburst, used to display a consecrated host for adoration.

mortal sin: A grave (serious) sin "which is also committed with full knowledge and deliberate consent"; as it "destroys charity" and "turns man away from God," it must be confessed before receiving Communion (see *Catechism of the Catholic Church*, 1854–64).

narthex: The area in a church between the main entrance and the nave, sometimes called the *gathering space* or *vestibule*; the gateway between the outside world and the church.

nave: The main body of the church's worship space where the congregation sits.

offertory: The part of the Mass when the gifts of bread and wine are brought to the priest to take to the altar.

pall: A white cloth used as a sacred covering (for example, for a casket or chalices).

paten: A small, platelike vessel for the host.

pew: A long wooden bench with a back; in a church, often placed in rows in the nave.

procession: An ordered and formal moving from one place to another as part of a ceremony or rite. The entrance procession is at the beginning of Mass; the final recession is at the end of Mass, after the final blessing and dismissal.

purificator: A small, folded linen cloth for wiping the chalice and Communion cups.

pyx: A small, round vessel with a lid used for carrying Communion to the sick and homebound.

Roman Missal, The: The official book of prayers for the Mass, once called the *Sacramentary*; it does not contain the readings, which are found in the *Lectionary* and the *Book of the Gospels*.

sacrarium: A sink draining into the ground for holy water to be disposed of carefully; it is used for the purification of vessels.

sacred vessels: The vessels used to hold the precious Body (ciborium) and the precious Blood (chalice).

sacristan: A person responsible for the preparations at Mass but who does not serve at the altar.

sacristy: A room used for preparation before Mass, where the priest vests and the sacred vessels are prepared.

sanctuary (chancel): A central, elevated space in a church reserved for ministers and their assistants; includes the altar, ambo, and celebrant's chair.

sanctuary lamp: A candle, usually red, that burns near the tabernacle to show that Christ is present.

seminarian: A man studying for the ordained priesthood; his school is called a *seminary.*

stole: A vestment worn by deacons and priests during Mass and other liturgical functions. A priest's stole hangs down the front over both shoulders; a deacon's stole is worn diagonally over the left shoulder like a sash.

surplice: A decorative white garment, like a shirt, that is put on over a cassock, only going down to the waist.

tabernacle: A large, decorated box with a lock that contains consecrated hosts. It's kept in a prominent place in church.

thurible (censer): A metal container with small openings attached to a set of chains; it is used for burning incense.

thurifer: The altar server or acolyte responsible for the incense.

venial sin: An action against the moral law that is a "less serious matter," or one that is a grave matter but is done "without full knowledge or without complete consent" (see *CCC* 1854–64).

vestibule: See **narthex**.

vestment: A religious garment worn by clergy and other ministers while performing their duties.

zucchetto: A skull cap worn by bishops and certain other clergy.

My Parish

My Parish Contacts

Who is in charge of altar servers at your parish? If you have questions, need help, or need to reschedule or find a replacement, call him or her first.

Altar Server Coordinator

Phone number

E-mail

Pastor / Deacon

Phone number

E-mail

Other

Phone number

E-mail

Other Altar Servers

Who are some altar servers you just met? Maybe you trained with them. Maybe they are more senior altar servers.

Other
_____

Phone number
_____

E-mail
_____

Other
_____

Phone number
_____

E-mail
_____

Other
_____

Phone number
_____

E-mail
_____

Other
_____

Phone number
_____

E-mail
_____

Other
_____

Phone number
_____

E-mail
_____

Notes on What to Do at My Parish

_____

_____

_____

_____

_____

_____

_____

_____

_____

_____

_____

_____

_____

_____

_____

_____

_____

Solutions to Activities

Crossword Solution (Pages 46-47)

		1.C							
		H				2.T			
	3.S	A	N	C	T	U	A	R	Y
		L				B			
		I				E			
		C		4.A		R			
	5.V	E	S	T	M	E	N	T	S
				B		A			
				O		C			
	6.P				7.A	L	B		
8.C	H	A	S	U	B	L	E		
	A				T				
	E				A				
9.C	I	N	C	T	U	R	E		

Scramble Solution (Pages 48-49)

1. P Y X
2. C I B O R I U M
3. C E N S E R
4. F L A G O N
5. D A L M A T I C
6. C R U E T
7. C O R P O R A L
8. G E N U F L E C T
9. P U R I F I C A T O R
10. C E L E B R A N T

Word Search Solution (Pages 50-51)

My First Mass as an Altar Server

✝

Name

_____

Date

_____

Feast / Occasion

_____

Parish / Location

_____

Priest / Celebrant

_____

Deacon / Concelebrant

_____

Other Server(s)

_____

Main Duties

_____

Memories

_____

_____

_____

_____

_____

_____

_____